MW01502705

FULL FACE TO THE LIGHT

FULL FACE TO THE LIGHT

Poems & Illuminations

by Marye Gail Harrison

Marye Gail Harrison

Antrim House
Simsbury, Connecticut

Library of Congress Control Number: 2012930034

ISBN: 978-1-936482-17-7

First Edition, 2012

Watercolor sketches by the author

Photographs of the author by John Benford
© 2011 John Benford (www.johnbenfordstudios.com)

Book Design by Rennie McQuilkin

Antrim House
860.217.0023
AntrimHouse@comcast.net
www.AntrimHouseBooks.com
21 Goodrich Road, Simsbury, CT 06070

*This book is dedicated to my parents
Marjorie and Sterling Harrison
who taught me to love deeply.*

ACKNOWLEDGMENTS

Some of the poems in this volume first appeared in the journal *Voices, The Seabury Trail Meditation Guide,* and *Glimpses of the Spirit,* often in earlier versions. Others first appeared in chapbooks entitled *Poems for Each Season* and *A Collection of Family Stories.*

I am grateful to Bev Spence for her proofreading and to my faithful friends who have listened to these poems as they were lived and written over many years. Thank you for all your love and support. I particularly thank Katharine Carle, who has led the Seabury Retirement Community poetry group year after year and without whom I might have given up writing and would never have met my editor and publisher. Rennie McQuilkin has awed me with his gentle understanding of what I was trying to say and his ability to help me say it more clearly. You gave me the best 70th birthday present I could ever have imagined, this volume which tells my story. Thank you so much.

Table of Contents

IV. FEEDING ON THE LIGHT

V. SWEET BREAD OF LIFE

Have patience with everything unresolved in your heart and try to love the questions themselves as if they were locked rooms or books written in a very foreign language. Don't search for the answers, which could not be given to you now, because you would not be able to live them. And the point is, to live everything. Live the questions now. Perhaps then, someday far in the future, you will gradually, without even noticing it, live your way into the answers.

from "Letters to a Young Poet," Ranier Maria Rilke

I. PRELUDE

GO FOR IT!

Go for it down the dark tunnel into light
     and air in lungs, into new creation,
     merging into new flesh-forms
     and being on Planet Earth.

Go for it past cautions from parents,
     teasing for being different,
     confusion of wanting to be in the culture and not being
     and confusion for being the culture, too.

Go for it past hormones lusting after intimacy,
     past fear of premature pregnancy,
     past first loves which you outgrew
     and didn't know how to end gracefully.

Go for it past first moving away from home,
     leaving anxious parents in pain
     and feeling guilty about leaving them.

Go for it past false starts,
     trying to try everything
     and not always learning
     from your mistakes.

Go for it past first marriage, children you nursed in the night
     when you were half asleep,
     past stories told and books read and questions answered,
     past rice cereal and applesauce

and diced bananas sticking to the high chair tray
and Cheerios picked up by stubby fingers,
stuffed into open wet mouths on sticky faces,
onto their faces, onto your face.

Go for it past backaches and claustrophobia
    and folding laundry and eating at McDonalds
    with other women and their children.

Go for it past at-home careers as volunteer and handicrafter,
    furniture refinisher and yoga teacher,
    past self-help books and adult ed courses,
    past trying to explain and not being able to.

Go for it past your first weekend without the kids
    and finding out how little
    you knew about yourself.

Go for it past cold feet, sleepless nights,
    stomach churning, black fear dreams
    and poems and journals
    which reek of panic at breaking out
    and panic at staying where you are.

Go for it on your own again
    but starting over too late,
    with many responsibilities,
    crying how hard it is and how lonely.

Go for it past friends who mean well
    but don't understand
    and don't support your strength.

Go for it into depths of consciousness
    where spirit exists,
    where light is self-knowledge
    and darkness is infinite opportunity to expand.

Go for it into integration of material human body
    and self
    with pure light.

Go for it in visions,
    voices in your dreams,
    and images in your mind of what life can be.

Go for it to a sense of your own mission,
    feel it settle solidly into your body and being,
    feel your heart supported by your loin power,
    claim all of yourself
    even that past understanding.

Go for it past judgment into acceptance of the whole,
    make room for a larger perspective
    which can show connections
    and give meaning in time.

Go for it wherever it leads
    and know I am with you,
    for I am going for it too.

II. FAMILY MATTERS

TASTE OF TENNESSEE SUMMERS

I can almost step out the low upstairs window when I wake up,
smelling smoky tobacco-fired morning
as roosters crow out past the red hollyhocks.
My cousin makes me buttery fried toast
with chewy blackberry jam,
salty bacon with a hard rind and canned grapefruit juice.

By noon the windows are closed, shades on the sunny sides;
only the porch swing is cool.
I hide in the dark pantry where the light chain is too high.
We eat dark pink country-cured ham
on fluffy biscuits made with lard.
I like fried bologna or pimento cheese salad on white bread.
Sweet tea.

Before supper washing up in the pan
with water from the pail filled at the pump,
I sip from the dipper like everybody else.
There's crispy fried chicken pulley bone
if I pick before Uncle Nathan,
creamy whipped potatoes,
fat butter beans with summer-ripe tomatoes,
fried corn with scorched bits from the iron skillet bottom,
have-another-hot-one
rolls or biscuits right from the oven
and warm fresh peach cobbler, bubbled over the crust.
"Y'all git enough to eat?"

After dark on the porch,
all the chairs rocking, glider swaying,
swing chains clinking, lightening bugs blinking,
adults laughing low, telling stories,
'til someone gently guides me
up to the slightly musty attic guest bed.
"Sweet dreams, sugar."

I KNOW IT'S TIME

Light winks at me from the leaves
by the small wooden bridge.
My little brown sandals make a funny sound
as I run over it.
Below me, water talks
but I don't know what it says
and I keep running.

I am surprised when Mommy comes up behind me
and asks breathlessly, "Where are you going?"
"Meet Daddy," I say.

I know this is the way we go
to meet him at the bus after work.
He will say, "How's my redhead?"
and scoop me into his arms.
Maybe he will let me play with his black lunchbox
if I am careful to take out the empty thermos bottle.

I know it's time to go find him.
(What inner clock tells a three-year-old?)
Knowing, I run to him, alone not fearing,
sure of the path as well as the time.

I would run to the bridge now
if only I could find the way.

ALL HIS LIFE

He was responsible all his life.
Chores on the farm early on
after walking home from football practice.
To pay his boarding house debt
when he married Mom,
he sold his car and walked to work
at J. C. Penney.
During the war, he worked in the hell holes
of the shipyard
so he wouldn't be drafted and leave us.
Never took a road job selling
so he could be home at night.
Protecting us, never risked it all
to invest in his own shoe store
as he had dreamed of doing.
Bigger stores promised by the chain
didn't come through.
His ulcer acted up,
sending him to bed
many nights after work.
Switching companies at 50
with less freedom and better benefits,
he took early retirement at 62.
Not understanding such sacrifices at 37,
I asked, "What'll mom do if you die first?"
"I've done the best I could do," he said softly,
not raising his eyes from the newspaper
to shame me.

A SWEET-SMELLING WAY

It was a bright spring morning when my Daddy died.
The air was filled with the sweet smell of honeysuckle.

Intoxicated by the smell and all my loving memories,
inside I heard him say to me,
"You must find a way
to show your love in your work,
more than I did."

And the air was filled
with sweet honeysuckle smell.

His heart finally broke that day into so many pieces
the surgeon couldn't put it back together.

"Find the light, Daddy.
Follow the light.
Oh God, Daddy.
Trust It."

And the air was filled...

"Yes, let him go.
He wouldn't want it the other way.
Let him go, peacefully."

"You must find a way to show your love..."

The sweet smell of honeysuckle.
"Let him go."
Sweet smell…
"Let him go, find a way."

Find a way…

BOOTS, BEANS, AND POEMS

"We won't be coming for dinner tonight,"
she called to explain.
"Why the hell not?" I responded.
"Hank's dead. Heart attack. I just got home."
I flew to her with inadequate arms
to tether her as she plunged into the black hole of grief
known to widows whose husbands die suddenly.
Beside her feet I saw his work boots,
still sweaty and muddy
from turning over their garden that morning.
How can he not be here
when his sweaty boots are here?

My father had just put in his garden days before
he died unexpectedly in open-heart surgery.
The strings to mark two rows of beans
ran neatly across the fresh furrows,
staked at each end by broken sticks.
By the time the funeral was over
the beans were up.
How can he not be here
when his beans are up?

It was three days ago this spring
when Dan died of a massive heart attack.
"I found the poems he was going to share tonight
at your spiritual reflections group.

It meant so much to him.
Could someone pick them up
so they'll be read?"
How can he not be here
when his poems are here?

We clean his boots,
We water and harvest his beans,
We read the poems he picked for us to hear.
Out of such small gestures
life slowly heals itself.

Dedicated to the widows - Barb, Mom and Chris

309 CHURCH STREET, LAST VISIT

I walk through your Tennessee house
before your move
looking at each room one more time,
hopefully through your eyes.
It's been a good place.
It's hard to let go.

Across the street,
beyond the cemetery,
the huge red sun marks another ending.
Walking over I pass Uncle Clarence,
Aunt Cullie and Ma Gardner,
and finally reach Daddy's grave.

I hear the train wheels rushing on rails
and its lonely whistle.

Who will find these headstones,
see what my parents loved,
and know my love put the bird and rose there
to mark a life, a love?

A small flock of geese comes honking over
and then three more,
right overhead.

It's been a good place.
It's hard to let go.

CEMETERY

I found Daddy and sat down in his shade,
leaned against his granite mass,
feeling grass and tears wet through.
"I miss you."

Old memories approach from the distance
howling *WooOO WA!   WooOO WA!*
Chased through town by
CLICKedyCLACK, CLICKedyCLACK, claang.
Nobody hardly stops anymore with "Hi dee do. How ya'll?"
Or even a wave.
It's all fainter now.
Woooo wa!   Woooo wa!

Gone with the dew.
Reckon I better
git going too.

HAIKU

spooning favorite ice cream
into mother's mouth
almost gone

RESURRECTION TIME

My mom was growing a white pine seedling
started in a plastic drinking cup
on her windowsill.
In the hospital for stomach surgery,
she reminded me to water it.

Recovering, she had been snoring
while I read next to her bed.
I didn't notice when her heart stopped.
Through my sobs they revived her.
Then she was full of tubes in ICU.
Grief filled me.
I prepared to let her go.

But this is spring, resurrection time.
She is back with us,
missing her little apartment,
as alive as her windowsill pine.

MOON FOR MOM

My 92-year-old mom was lying in the hospital bed,
rubbing her hands around her distended belly, enormous
on her 95-pound body.
"What's in there?" she said.
"I think you swallowed the moon."
"Looks like it," she chuckled.

No more surgery to try to fix it, she stated clearly over
and over. She was ready to die. She'd had a long, good life
she said and she was grateful but ready to go, unafraid.
Gracefully, with resolution, she counseled all who
questioned her.

From her hospital room on the 12th floor, her only view
was abstract art at best — the lower two thirds was grey
water-stained building ledge, above it a slash of sky. She
loved nature with its rich greens, bright flowers and
colorful birds; I was disappointed for her.

That night she asked what the round white light in the
window was. "Oh, it's the moon," she murmured as she
turned her whole body toward it. She was still watching
it with a little smile on her lips, stomach-pumping tube
running out her nose, when I left later that night. Life
gives you lemons, make lemonade — that's how she lived.

Disconnected from all the tubes and discharged to
a nursing home for hospice care a few days later, she

wondered if she could see the moon from her new room. We celebrated the next night when the almost full moon emerged from behind a tower right into view from her bed.

The following two nights were cloudy. She was waning more quickly than the moon now, tolerating only ice chips, red popsicles, and warm sweet tea with milk.

When the moon finally emerged it was behind a blue spruce and too far to the left for her to see. Gathered at her bedside at 9 p.m., the evening nurse, mom's best friend, my step daughter and I were all frustrated. Mom was too weak to stand or even use the wheel chair, although her mind was still as lucid as the moonlight.

Inspired by a friend's story, I took the large mirror off the wall where it hung over a bureau and turned it toward her. In the darkness, the reflected moon traveled like a pale white spot light on the wall behind her bed.

I aimed it onto her face. There she shone in the moonlight, smiling. In her eyes, I could see tiny moons gleaming back to me.

Five days later, Mom died peacefully on a beautiful morning with the sun shining in her window.

A MOTHER'S GIFT

I nursed each of my sons six months.
I can still see the first one's bright eyes looking up at me,
never breaking contact
as I lifted the nipple of my full moon breast
into his soft wet mouth.

Later, in the heat of those close moments
the younger one's eyes would close
while sweat swelled on his temples and lips,
mouth automatically sucking
as he dropped off to sleep in my arms.

Later, having lost myself,
I left them with their father.
As they found themselves,
they went their own ways.

I wish I could give them something now
that would nourish us all again.

HOLEY JEANS

Every vacation he came home
from college
he brought two pairs of holey jeans
for me to salvage.

At first, hand-mending worked.
Then I used my sewing machine
to zigzag stitch
the growing gaps.

His last year, I lined them
with madras Bermudas from Goodwill,
amazingly solid where
the jeans were not.

Our relationship had been rent asunder
when I'd left him with his father too young.
I was trying to sew us back together.

POINT REYES LIGHT

Three hundred fifty is the number on the step
at the top of the cliff, the steps
curving down to the restored lighthouse,
a little over ten for each of your thirty years,
almost six for each of my sixty,
plunging down to the Pacific
with only rails, wire fencing and better judgment
to contain us. In the late afternoon sun
bright reflection turns the water dark, impenetrable.
Behind us, grasshopper-colored meadows
roll away treeless to isolated farms.
To the south, like a tropical mirage, translucent aqua
unites the amber cliffs and cerulean sky.

We go down together after our long ride,
when I listened truly to your long-pent feelings.
Knowing how precious every moment is with you,
I keep my worries to myself.
I have this one day with you, my firstborn son.
Yet in the lighthouse something pulls me away
from the guide's stories. I say I need to start back
and for you to come when you are ready.

After the first hundered steps I rest on a bench.
I breathe hard, thinking how you told me today
how angry you are with me —
how I failed you when I left you at ten with your father
and too much responsibility.

I climb on to where the sun's brilliance blinds me
and stop at step two hundred.
Directly below, waves crash on rocks,
constant churning my gut recognizes.
I hear you say you felt at twelve
you had no real mother, that after my new marriage
my home no longer felt like safe harbor to you.

Climbing again, I know at step three hundred
I will make it, but I stop, in no hurry now,
surrounded by the rusty rock faces of the cliff,
marveling at the little gardens clinging in the cracks
but recalling the grimace that scarred your face
as you said I was oblivious to your daily humiliation
in high school, an honor student in AP classes
anguished behind the mask of your long blond hair.

I slow my pace and take the last fifty steps more easily.
Looking back, I see you have not started up yet.
At the top I lean on the rail to the south,
feeling the nurturing hot sun and cool breeze
as I search my own horizon for understanding, for peace.
I hold your story as I once held you in my womb,
a living part of me
ready, I trust, to birth itself in its own time.

Alone here, I first see her far below me,
a long dark oval just under the surface,
living gem in aqua setting,
her powerful body guarding her calf from the open sea.
As they slowly glide past

joy sprays me like mist from their blow holes,
and then they are gone.
The cold sad shadow of your missing them passes over.
Then great love widens me as I embrace both joy and grief.

When you join me on the edge, I describe the whales
and we watch seven seals undulate past.
I so wish I had shielded you longer from life's open waters
so you could play more like the seals.
Immersed now in deeper waters, we are at last ready
to move on.

COME IN FROM THE RAIN

"Come in from the rain
to the warmth of my arms," he said.
"I will talk to you with my hands
and you can listen with your body."

Years later after his stroke,
he still spoke to me.
Years later, I could still hear him
in the silence of his touch.

SPRING THAW

As the mini ice age of seasonal winter recedes,
primordial pools fill the swamp.
First life emerges dark purple, chartreuse-speckled
with swollen turrets like Turkish temple tops
and bright green towers soon spiraling above.
In the meadow swamp maples'
tiny red buds flower
from otherwise bare branches.

On rivulets after rain
the mallard murmurs low warnings toward the rushes
formally dressed in iridescent emerald cap,
white starched collar,
his "means business" spring suit.
At the edge of the trail a rabbit freezes,
a ball of fur and fear as I approach,
holds still until I am well away.

Meanwhile another ice age descends
on my eighty-year-old husband.
Not a meteor in the Yucatan
like the one that extinguished dinosaurs
but a stroke in his beautiful brain
freezes his exuberant expressions,
expands, slow and determined,
crushing all in its path.

"Shit, shit," he grumbles
as I announce his shower time.
"Precisely," I say cheerily —
"where's my Mr. Clean?"
"He has shuffled away," he murmurs.

HOW'S HE DOING?

He rarely talks now
and when he does he repeats himself.
Sometimes I ask him
"What are you thinking about?"
"I think about death a lot."

Sometimes he shouts, stammering
"You don't understand!
I don't have the intelligent...mind...
I'm not what I was!"

But yesterday after my poetry class
while he waited for me to make his lunch
he asked me for the first time
if I would read him some of my poems.

For almost an hour I read him poems
about my mother and father.
He took his handkerchief from his pocket,
still folded in quarters, to wipe his eyes.

"What are you feeling now?" I ask.
"All the losses.
All the losses."

OLDER LOVE

Our bodies savor touching
bare skin to bare skin;
its been a long time.
What I feel is not the old passion.
Something sweeter, wiser,
sadder, gentler fills me.
Our touching glides past angry hurtful years,
caresses the losses of early dementia,
kisses away the pain of not living together.

On a summer day at the vacation cottage,
gratitude for what we have left
shimmers in the sunlight streaming onto the bed.
On the way back
we stop for an Italian dinner,
sharing a glass of wine
to toast our love
ever evolving.

III. Reaching for the Light

IV. FEEDING ON THE LIGHT

IN MY NEW NEIGHBORHOOD

In my new neighborhood
on clear mornings
above dawn's rosy arousal
two morning stars await the sun and me.

In my new neighborhood
royal blue lupine tower like castle turrets
lording over their common cousins,
the purple vetches.

In my new neighborhood
finches in golden summer uniforms
advance with ebony epaulettes
to ravish the fluff from thistle tufts.

In my new neighborhood
young milkweed renounces
her coiffured globe of mauve blossoms
for a nun's simple beige habit,
until winds toss it back
to blow awry her white old woman hair.

In my new neighborhood
at sunset above the hill,
peppermint stripes linger in light blue,
sweet ending after dinner mints.

In my new neighborhood
courting fireflies brightly blink,
dancing late as meadow's Milky Way
to cricket music on warm June nights.

In my new neighborhood
full moon slides out slowly to stand alone,
sumptuously announcing itself.
I smile to greet my old friend's face
here in my new neighborhood.

HAIKU II

Take a walk
clear your head—maybe
something will come to you

FALL IS ENDING

Fall is ending.
The bright leaves are down,
many branches are gray and bare.
The air this morning is crisp and cold.
I dread facing winter.

John is facing his fears about his health.
He worked hard to retire
and now he feels his body has failed him.
He has searched for God
and says he prays for help.
But so far
there seems little comfort for him.

Carolyn, facing her own health problems
concluded there was no reason
to do anything
but exactly what she wanted
because no matter what one's health,
life is so short.

So how do we make sense of our lives?

I am watching
the grey titmice at my feeder.

LEAVES FALLING

Leaves falling in my yard —
oak, ash, maple, birch
mixed with white pine needles,
rust, gold, lime, tan,
a mat of confusion,
residue of finished things.

Rustling under my feet,
you call out to me,
cluttering my path
grabbing my focus with your
floating forms,
riotous colors,
noisy confusion,
whispering messages,
whirling me into your chaos,
piled between me
and the stark bare cleansing of winter.
You are interrupting me.

When I took fall leaves to my son in Texas
he kissed them
and mounted them on the windows.
As a child I raked leaves into piles
and jumped and hid in them,
reveling in the musty scent,
not knowing the smell of death and decay.

I need to kiss these leaves of mine,
jump in and hide in piles of them.
I am not ready yet for winter bareness.

COMING TO DARKNESS

This is the time of darkness when the nights lengthen
and drive us into the dark voids inside ourselves.
We falter in face of bare trees and icy winds.
Thick blankets of gray clouds offer no warmth.
I am aware of the thinness of my defenses
and vulnerable, I shiver in the cold outside
and the vast darkness within.

Where does the courage come from to light candles
and decorate, to celebrate and feast?
I know, of course, that spring comes again.
Still I pause a moment on this edge, unsure,
not of the nature outside me but of the nature within.

Where is the peace in my darkness?
Where is the restoration that precedes the surge
of new growth? I am not sure.
I busy myself outwardly and avoid looking within,
yet I am never fooled.
My doubts are always there like the void behind me
into which I resist moving.

Move back.
Move back into that void.
Step into the darkness.
Gently move through the resistance. Back. Back.
My spine straightens as I am filled with quiet strength —
dark strength from the enormous black void
where all life begins.

Now I light my candles to intensify the darkness.
Not to defy the dark but in acceptance of it.
I do not have to resolve the tension
between the dark and light.
I contain them both.

And as I open the doors to the advent,
it is myself I open to the dark peace within.

LONG BLUE SHADOWS

As I drove past the hilly pastureland, I saw clearly the long
blue shadows on the snowy unscarred hillside
cast by the sun from the spine of the cedar
and the bare branches
of the maple.

Light of Understanding cast forward the long blue shadow
of my life that I might see it clearly before me
on the bare white expanse
of this moment.

WINTER DAY
IN BLACK AND WHITE

Against jumble of thoughts
which thrash in my mind,
a bare winter tree's shape
is peaceful, benign.

Against light grey sky
and new spacious snow,
I see silhouette of hawk glide
and profile of crow.

SNOW DAY

Snow days are gifts of spacious time:
regular routine cancelled days,
no pressure days,
no agenda days,
quiet, calming down days,
daydream in warm shawl days,
popcorn and good book,
cocoa, favorite nook days.

On my snow day I do laundry,
make spaghetti sauce for supper,
catch up on email,
clean off my desk,
write overdue thank-you notes.

Writing this poem
saves the day.

CATTAILS IN FEBRUARY

Cattails in a frozen swamp
on a mild February noon
amidst blue sky, cold air and bright sun.
I grab a cattail in my hand
and it erupts, uncurling itself
in graceful rolling waves of foaming fluff.
These catch the breeze
and float off, ignited by the sun.
I smile and grab more and more,
carefree in releasing play.

My life feels compressed and dry
on stalks of habits
rooted in a frozen swamp of fear.
I wait for a gentle hand
to playfully release me
that I might freely float
in February air.

MARCH HAWKS

Each day above tree line
in March's crisp blue air,
two hawks soar slowly, then turn
white underbellies flashing sunlight,
swoop down, nearly careening
in tango tension.
My thoughts follow them.
Wings wide after winter waiting,
feathers flared, I long to rise
above still snowy meadows
in search of life.

Deep inside me
in a field of stillness,
another pair of hawks,
doubt and desire,
arise in dramatic dance,
stealing my present attention.
Once I name them, I notice
they glide out of sight.
I am at peace again.

HAIKU III

sun lit hawk wings
flashing mirror signals
spring forecast

SPRING SONG

In the warm sun of a cool March day,
a small gray bird calls out over and over,
calls out sitting on a maple branch
bulging with spring flower buds.
From across the way, each time
the call is answered,
over and over.

And in the tall blue spruce
on a platform of branches near the trunk,
the mourning dove lowers her head
and drops her wings to her side.
She lifts her rump as high as she can,
quivering with the strain of it,
tail straight up like an exclamation point.
The male slips from branch to branch
closer and closer.
He sniffs her ovarian sweetness,
each pecks the other's bobbing head…

I too call out over and over
often in the warm sun on a cool spring day
to Something across the way.
I too lift myself up,
straining inwardly, and whisper to the day
"Come to me! Come to me!"

FLASHES

Sometimes on my daily walk, my longing
for the feeling of oneness
that I imagine comes with enlightenment
drops away in the flashes —
cardinal red winging across verdant lawns,
white back of flying flicker,
goldfinch yellow and black
streaking away from saffron coreopsis
still bobbing from the lift-off.
Suddenly I hear birdcalls everywhere,
louder than the murmur of distant traffic,
louder than the thoughts that drive me.
In that flash, before I even name it *Beauty*,
I am simply there.

SIGNAL LIGHTS

car off road   blink blink
fireflies in field   blink blink

RUGOSA ROSES

Rugged rugosa roses,
pricker stems —
thick wild rose scent
clots at the back of my throat
when I bend close.
Five floppy petals like
ladies' garden party hats,
fuchsia pink, crowned
by golden stamen halo
when newly opened.
Bumblebees ravish
this glowing center.
Passionate bellies rub
in agitated circles
gathering essence,
then out, then back again
for just one more merging.
Once more. Once more.

FEEDING ON THE LIGHT

I move my meditation chair to the window,
where reflected red and yellow glow
of October maples bathes me in sunset pink.
I strain to absorb this moment
until inner silence takes me.
As I sit in the leaves' radiance,
they penetrate directly
and like the first photosynthetic cells
four billion years ago,
I learn to feed on the light.

SEPTEMBER SUNFLOWERS

It was just a month ago
that the maiden sunflowers
lifted their brown faces surrounded by ruffled sunbonnets
to the morning sun in unison,
proud in their glory.

Now their leaves are shriveled.
Their heavy faces turn down to the earth,
leaving their spines doubled over.
They cannot lift their ripe heads.
They can only hope the sun will find their curved backs
and warm them.

Like the birds that peck at their seed eyes,
you take a shed tear into your mouth.
Cracking it open between your teeth,
you savor the truth kernel from the old crone sunflower
so that each day, with spine straight,
you will turn full face to the light.

INTO THE FLOW

Some scientists say the heart is not a pump
and the blood knows how to move itself,
only regulated by the heart.
If so, then maybe I also know when to move.
Maybe I feel summer's impulses
signaling squirrels mating,
cardinals singing,
daisies blooming,
maples leafing,
grass greening,
streams rushing.
Into this flow I go,
knowing my way in the larger confluence,
moving with it
as though floating
on a big inner tube platelet
in the life stream river,
buoyed by knowing
gurgling and babbling messages,
telling of the irises, butterflies and deer
as well as the chute, the vortex, the pool.
And my heart regulates my going on,
downstream, to the sea.

V. SWEET BREAD OF LIFE

BIG SKIES

Watching the light blue sky and peach clouds
darken at sunset behind gray-blue clouds,
I remember the first time I really noticed the sky.
Almost thirty, I was heading west from New England
for ten weeks on my first camping trip.
In the plains states, I was nervous.
Day after day passed without familiar enclosure
by eastern hills and forests.
The sky had grown too huge too quickly.
Living out under it with my husband and child
made me anxious.
Rocky Mountain National Park saved me for a while
though I couldn't say from what.
But storm clouds in Arizona broke into me.
Rigidly I watched as huge thunderheads roiled up,
deep multi-layered gray blankets
moving faster and faster,
leaving pale streamers shattered, flowing behind.
At the campground rest room, I heard women talking
about hail stones big as golf balls.
Outside again, walking back to our unprotected tent,
I watched the clouds as though for enemy planes.
Put up the dining fly (surely the hail would tear it down!)
or not? Each delay made me more frantic.
As the sky darkened and light faded
I imagined my toddler struck by lightning.
I thought maybe we could all three sleep in the station wagon.
"Let's make a picnic in the tent!" my husband said.
"We'll spread the table cloth on the floor

and bring the cooler in.
We'll have sandwiches and cold drinks
and snuggle together warm and dry."
Reframed options zapped my mind like lightning.
New possibilities rolled like thunder
across my parched experience
shaped by years under smaller skies.
The smell of fear dissipated
as I embraced the weather, laughing.
I spread a little freedom of thought
like a rare paté on my usual fare.
Ever since that taste of freedom
I have been starved for big skies.

HAIKU IV

forced forsythia
some branches bloom
some don't

I KNOW I NEED SACRED TIME

I know I need sacred time.
I know I need sacred space.

I cleared my calendar to create more time.
I even have a space I can use.
Why don't I nourish myself?

I go to the kitchen and snack.
I wander through piles of mail.
I look over half finished projects.
I file a few things, browse a while.
I check my email and answer it.

I know I need sacred time.
I know I need sacred space.
Why don't I nourish myself?

There's a big SHOULD in my way.
I should "get everything done" on my list first.
Sacred time is not on my list.

I know I need sacred time.
I know I need sacred space.

Why don't I nourish myself?

WINGS

The morning sun almost blinded me
but still I watched the pair of soaring hawks
until I had to move along to make the light.
Returning that way later
I saw a large dead bird in the road.
One wing stretched up from its smashed body,
a final monument to life's gift.
My heart wrenched, remembering the soaring hawks.
I ached for the wing fluttering now in the wind.
A quail it was; I took some loosened tail feathers
then came back again,
scooped up the bird's remains
and took them home.
I wanted the wings.

I cut them off before I buried the carcass.
The flesh on the wings was still red.
Spread open, the large feathers were dark brown suede.
At the shoulder was a cluster of small jewels,
ovals of amber set in copper and onyx.
I nailed the outstretched wings to the garage to dry.
On the third day when I went to check,
they were gone!
Some of the jewels were scattered nearby
but the open wings were gone.

Some other bird, perhaps a hawk,
had scavenged too, had coveted those wings.
"They were mine," I wanted to shout.
Nature has its own ways.
Those wings were not mine to possess
yet they had moved my soul and I kept
the spirit of them.

If I am to soar, I'll have
to find my own wings.

FROM WONDER WOMAN TO CRONE

Our confirmations
  weddings and
  birthday celebrations
are pale remnants of what we need for our souls.
We long for the richness of ancient tribal rites
to bring forth the Crone.

"Harsh name, sounds like a witch. Too strong."
"Right!"

Long ago we were called from innocence.
Something broke into our early playhouses, hurt us
and gave us our first taste of growth.
We read of Wonder Woman and wished for her magic bracelets
to protect us.

We felt alone and violated.
We taught ourselves to accommodate so we could survive.
Often in secret, in private hours stolen from responsibilities,
some taught themselves forbidden skills.
  Some taught themselves to hunt and fish.
  Some to fight and some to run.
  Some to read and write.
  Some to dance and sing.
  Some to analyze and reason.
  Some to lead.
  Some to change the way it is.
"Is there something wrong with me?

My happy marriage and home,
my children and volunteer activities are not enough."

"Wait until your children are grown
and your husband's career is stable,
then you can grow.
Take these three times a day;
you won't feel anything while time passes you by.
It is wrong for you to put yourself before the others."

Many of us slept through those years with Valium.
And some are still asleep.

There were other ways of coping —
   food and alcohol addictions
   love affairs
   hurting our children and husbands
   card games, crafts and gardening,
   at-home careers.

All that plus 9 to 5 jobs
and burnout schedules,
making sure no one did without, but us.

Remember, each trial is an initiation.

Allies came still later —
   self-help books,
   support groups and exercise classes,
   massage therapy and rebirthing,
   crystals, herbs and meditation,

journals and art classes.

Where can my cup overflow?
We are the lucky ones, in middle class America.
What of the poor women here and elsewhere who use
    themselves up by age 35,
just surviving?
What right have I to complain or be dissatisfied?

But they are waging war again
and pollution is making us sick.
Life is out of balance. Not just mine.
The earth is dying. Not just me.
What can I do? I am only a woman.
I am only one woman.

"I wish to claim my crone power. How do I prepare?"

We fast from fast foods which are hard to digest.
Plants nourish us more.

We study ancient wisdom and meditate on the Single
    Source of All,
expanding our awareness.

We exchange our old uniform
    for more natural clothes, looser,
    less underwear and makeup,
    deeper scents,
    long earrings and many beads around our necks.
Our shoes are flat.

We can wiggle our toes and run and walk in these.
Our reading is serious.
About a new order of things.
About taking stands based on values.

We join with other women in classes and meetings,
over coffee or for lunch
to tell our stories
and to share our longings.

We rearrange our lives to make time.
We throw away accumulations.
We let our families do more for themselves.
We resign from groups that no longer fit well.
We reduce our working hours if we can.

We discipline ourselves in the new time we've made.
We meditate, exercise, read, bask in nature, and think.
We choose, create, act, reevaluate, adjust
and choose again.

Our awareness deepens.
Outside you may not see any differences.
Inside we are changed forever.
Our children no longer say "Get a life, Mom,"
but rather ask us what we're reading now
and install new software for us.

Our husbands are mystified at first.
Then they either smile and fall in love anew with us
or let us go to ease their sense of fear.

We need the celebration.
We have broken through and haven't noticed it
until now. Our wings grew on the inside.
We feel them flutter near our hearts
when our awareness quickens.

So let us gather together with poems and candles,
wash naked in natural waters and
walk to the edge at sunrise,
bring baskets of shells and feathers and stones
gathered along the way,
set them by the stack of books which inspire us,
sing and dance in a circle
and laugh until we can't see.
And let us invite our loved ones.
They need to be here to celebrate with us
even if they really don't understand,
especially if they don't.

We will read our poems and stories
and hang our art work all around,
put streamers in our hair
and sprinkle ourselves with flower petals and glitter.
We will anoint each other with scented oils,
massage our bodies,
especially our hands and feet
which have worked so hard to bring us here.
We will prepare treats to eat with love.
We will take rods and staffs to walk and lead with,
to use as talking sticks in council.
We will plant trees in our names

and scatter seeds for the birds.
For we have become Crones.

"Harsh name, sounds like a witch. Too strong."
"Right!"

Dedicated to Carolyn, written for all of us

BREAD OF LIFE

at the Genesis Retreat Center

Like yeasty dough
I began by resting in a warm place,
expanding organically.
Daily my spiritual baker checked me,
led me inward to know
deeply my simple whole flour and water,
blessed with yeast of life,
sweetened with honey.
A plump masseuse with sure wise hands
punched me down, kneaded me well,
releasing my sighs, sobs and belly laughs,
so I heard the still small voice within.
For days and days I baked and baked
until a fine golden crust formed
protecting moist freshness.
This is my body, which is given for me.
My body, the mother I had been looking for,
sweet bread of life.

MOUNTAIN BREATHING

I was having trouble breathing,
trudging up the wet, stony mountain path,
post-menopausal, out of shape, everything harder now.
I remembered how my one-breasted, one-lunged friend
taught me to breathe like mountain climbers at high altitudes.
Focus on the exhale, force the air out,
blow noisily through your lips,
wheww…
wheww…
Tie it to your steps — the rhythm makes it easy.

Wounded many ways,
we find ourselves seeking higher altitudes.
The air is thin, the way is steep,
our bodies not in shape for it,
yet here we are, drawn irresistibly upward.
Walking alone now or with old friends
who won't think our noisy breathing
and our strange pacing are embarrassing,
we celebrate just being on the path.
Wounded, set aside, we find our own reasons
to go up the trail.
Wounded ones, we teach each other to keep on climbing.

As we hike up the days of our lives,
release… exhale… expel… let go,
what we need to take in
will come on its own with little effort.

Left step, *wheww*, right step...
Left step, *wheww*, right step...
climbing to the top for the view,
hoping to see at least seven shades of blue.

EYE OF THE LOTUS

In the silence in the eye of the lotus
in the center of my heart
is a sacred void,
the space between
my breathing in and my breathing out.
This lens looking in and looking out
is the eye of God by which God sees me
and I see God,
opening to billions of years of emerging truth
still unfolding to billions of possibilities —
including willful, irreversible destruction.

In the nanosecond I open my eyes,
in the nanosecond I live and breathe,
what do I will with my vision?

A TREE IN ME

At the beginning of each season of my life,
ideas of God sprout like spring leaves
and offer a summer of comforting shade.

At the end of each season of my life,
the outgrown gods turn and fall.

Sometimes in the bareness of winters,
I have called out to my old God,
saying how much I miss Him.

Now I long to strip away my outer bark,
to know deep inside my trunk
something — essential, still and peaceful,
even when the ground gives way beneath my roots,
and beyond my branches, winds of change
blow away my sky.

THE EDGE

My essential aloneness
tears at my heart
and tears flow across the aching.

What hell to have so many to love
and to have so many who loved me
and yet to face the edge alone.

Where can I gather up the strength
to move through the blackness
beyond the edge
if there is no comfort
in love and in friends.

Only I can be with me
at all times, in all places,
through all needs and feelings.

It seems so inadequate.
I fail myself as well as others
who will also face the edge alone.
I cannot go with you
and you cannot come with me.

We move into darkness alone
or we do not move at all.
Those are the only choices.

STRINGS OF MY HEART

My doctor's face winced
when he did a routine check of my heart:
"You've developed quite a murmur."
A year later things got more serious.

It was my strings.
Who knew heart valves have them like parachutes?
Isn't "Zing! went the strings..." just a song?
Who knew they can be broken like broken hearted melody?
Who knew it was bad for our heart to grow larger?
Isn't big-hearted good?

All I knew was I needed open heart surgery
to fix my mitral valve, which had broken strings,
causing my blood to wash backwards,
my heart to enlarge dangerously.
All I knew was dad had died at 72 in open heart surgery.
They were going to saw open my body, cut open my heart.
Although I'd had heart break like anyone else,
I was not prepared for this.

Art, a collage, brought me out of the terror.
Suddenly I felt a strong love for myself.
I was the mother of my own body.
I would lovingly give myself the very best care.
So I began to let go of old heart aches
in therapy, massage and spiritual retreats.
Harder was letting in all the love that flowed to me.
It came as pots of flowers,

as a prayer shawl knitted with "thoughts of you in every stitch,"
as Maryland crab cakes,
as a "love line" bag of gifts — a hankie, a heart pin,
a semi precious stone, a Mary Oliver poem
I read over and over.
My Albanian friend advised
"Do not entertain the uninvited guests
of doubt and fear."

My older son called to say
he was not ready to lose me,
that I might not be at his hoped-for wedding.
Much got healed that night on a long distance line,
and before we hung up, we could say clearly
"I love you."

Awareness changed as the time drew nearer:
I watched intent as a glowing golden spider
lit by glaring lights buried near landscaped trees
mended the swinging silver strands in her delicate web.
Guided by relaxation tapes, I imagined myself healed.
I saw myself swinging in our woven hammock,
drinking southern sweet tea in a cool breeze,
shy blue morning glories climbing the rails,
pots overflowing with flamboyant pink petunias.

My sons tethered me, relaying messages
which floated about like bright birthday balloons.
At 5 a.m. as we walked to the hospital,
knitted yarns of my prayer shawl
gently wrapped my husband and me.
Mars shone brightly over the dark buildings.

I pared down to go — no purse, empty pockets,
no watch, bracelet, or wedding rings.
Knowing friends and family far and near
held me in their hearts,
I hugged myself tightly in the shawl.
Finally I gave away even that.
A nurse held my hand in the cold operating room.

Waking hours later, I couldn't breathe.
I went under again, then surfaced
to soothing music on my son's MP3.
The doctor had succeeded in repairing my valve,
said it had looked like a smile when it closed.
He had removed calcium deposits,
making me more soft-hearted,
had stitched where the strings were broken
and inserted a ring for support —
to make me more stout-hearted.

I wept when I first saw the long incision
and huge purple bruises like eggplants covering my breasts.
And then, amazingly,
my body knew how to absorb that dark blood,
to heal itself.

It was a perfect day when I lay in my hammock
with my morning glories and petunias.
I cried for the goodness of my life.
I floated in a mysterious web of love.

Over time, tests showed my heart had grown smaller,
but in truth, my heart is bigger than ever.

COSMIC BIRTHDAY PARTY

The battery-operated bubble machine ran wild
all day in the yard. The kite was hung ornamentally
from low tree branches, its long
colorful streamers dancing with the breeze,
welcoming the afternoon guests.
Banners of planets and stars flapped from the deck,
beckoning the party-goers to sit in outer space.
Bouquets of white hydrangeas held center court
on assorted table cloths
inherited from her mother and aunts.

It was her seventieth birthday.
She, her kids, grandkids and close friends
all wanted to party —
Here's your last big decade,
better go for it while you can.
They liked bossing her out of the kitchen
as they prepared huge bowls of fruit and salads.
She was left alone in her party clothes,
all dressed up and no place to go,
remembering the funny birthdays
she'd once planned for them.

Everyone wore crazy head gear —
frog and crab, monkey and pirate hats,
hiking hats adorned with Hawaiian leis or weird buttons,
and one lavender wig.
An artist friend face painted embellished eyebrows,
beautiful and alien, on most everyone.

The birthday dessert was cosmic chocolate cupcakes
with chocolate ice cream, whipped cream and nuts,
all based on the proper proportion
of dark matter and energy
and visible atoms in the universe.
She told them ten percent of their body weight
was 13.8-billion-year-old hydrogen
created at the Big Bang.
That made her feel both wise and young.
Before singing Happy Birthday
and making wishes for her
as they blew out the candles on their cosmic cakes,
they read a poem together —
"Out of the stars have we come."

She had dressed up as "Madame Super Nova,"
told fortunes for those brave enough to face their futures,
tapping her black plastic fingernail
left over from Halloween
on the charms laid out for them to contemplate.

After a water balloon fight,
the boys, ages 8 to 55, played pick-up soccer.
The ringer was the only girl, age 13,
which caused the women on the sidelines
to kick around a few knowing smiles.

Near the end, they turned tables on their mother,
used her old party gags against her
to lead her laughing on a merry goose chase
with flashlights to find a stash of presents,
which showed her they had really understood renewal
of her interest in art.

After most went home
the real stars came out on night's dark banner
and the crickets took over the field to play.
Her daughter got out her more serious magic,
stroked and rang her set of brass bowls,
filling the soft summer air with ancient vibrations of spheres.
She checked their chakras with a pendulum.
Everyone was perfectly balanced, their faces aglow
with cosmic light.

ABOUT THE AUTHOR

A unt Marye, for whom Marye Gail Harrison is named, said she didn't know where in their family's Tennessee history Marye Gail got her story-telling ability. Perhaps it was from holding forth as an only child with her loving mother and father in Maryland, where she was raised. She was a good student, particularly influenced in the arts by Mrs. Rose in grade four and in writing by Mrs. Gira in high school. She won a scholarship to Pembroke College in 1959, majored in American literature, earned room and board by helping care for four children, and married the day after she graduated.

In the late 1970s when her two sons were still young, changes in women's culture and stirrings in herself she didn't understand contributed to a divorce and agreement that her children would live with their school teacher father. Afterwards, as she began her corporate career, she married an older man who mentored her and shared her love of the arts. She gained two very special step-daughters and their families as well. In 2003, she and her husband moved to a retirement community where they still reside.

She has been a social worker in the North End of Hartford, a wife and mom, a local Unitarian church leader, and after receiving her M.S. in Organizational Behavior in 1981, a corporate officer in financial services. She retired early and completed a two-year study to become a Spiritual Director.

Besides writing and painting, she likes surprises, slips into a southern accent on occasion, and tells fortunes as "Madam Super Nova." Her future is said to include more cosmic poems and paintings.

This book is set in Garamond Premier Pro, which had its genesis in 1988 when type-designer Robert Slimbach visited the Plantin-Moretus Museum in Antwerp, Belgium, to study its collection of Claude Garamond's metal punches and typefaces. During the mid-fifteen hundreds, Garamond—a Parisian punch-cutter—produced a refined array of book types that combined an unprecedented degree of balance and elegance, for centuries standing as the pinnacle of beauty and practicality in type-founding. Slimbach has created an entirely new interpretation based on Garamond's designs and on comparable italics cut by Robert Granjon, Garamond's contemporary.

To order additional copies of this book
or other Antrim House titles, contact the publisher at

Antrim House
21 Goodrich Rd., Simsbury, CT 06070
860.217.0023, AntrimHouse@comcast.net
or the house website (www.AntrimHouseBooks.com).

•

On the house website
in addition to information on books
you will find sample poems, upcoming events,
and a "seminar room" featuring supplemental biography,
notes, images, poems, reviews, and
writing suggestions.